Medical, Genetic & Behavioral Risk Factors of GORDON SETTERS

BY: ROSS D. CLARK, DVM

H. DAVID HAYNES, DVM – LEAD RESEARCH
AND EDITORIAL ASSISTANT
ART J. QUINN, DVM, DACVO – PROFESSOR EMERITUS,
OKLAHOMA STATE UNIVERSITY CENTER
FOR VETERINARY HEALTH SCIENCES
BRAD HOWARD, DVM – RESEARCH ASSISTANT
PAUL SCHMITZ, DVM – TECHNICAL ASSISTANT
JAN COODY, MBA – TECHNICAL ASSISTANT
NITA RITSCHEL – EXECUTIVE ASSISTANT
GERI HIBBLEN JACKSON – PHOTO ACQUISITIONS
LINDA A. CLARK, RVT, AKC JUDGE – PHOTO ACQUISITIONS

To order additional copies of this book or other
breed books of the 179 AKC recognized breeds by
this author, contact: Xlibris
1-888-795-4274
www.Xlibris.com Orders@Xlibris.com

MEDICAL, GENETIC & BEHAVIORAL RISK FACTORS OF GORDON SETTERS

INSIDE:

BY: ROSS D. CLARK, DVM

PREFACE

This book provides you with a through description and positive attributes of this breed including origin, purpose, history, normal heights and weights, acceptable colors and behavioral traits. Our books differ from most books on dog breeds because this book also provides you with a comprehensive and authoritative source of all the known predisposed hereditary health syndromes for the breed. You will find extensive references for each problem described. We also provide the breed club address for this breed and a list of laboratories and organizations that can provide professional help and information.

As a small animal veterinarian, I have always been intrigued by the way dogs have been bred to fill a purpose in life and further impressed that they also tend to love performing that service. Greyhounds and other sight hounds are built for speed with aerodynamic bodies consisting of small head, deep chest, narrow waist and large leg muscles. On the other hand Dachshunds take their name from German words meaning "badger dog" and they use their long nose, long body and short legs to both track, enter and dig into badger dens.

After developing a practice that catered to clients with show dogs, my interest in each breed continued to grow as I studied and observed more and more about the unique predisposition and incidence of health problems in each breed. Breeders of purebred dogs for show were a challenge and inspirational for me to research and help them with their unique health problems. Historically references to hereditary problems are scattered throughout various Veterinary medical texts and journals such as ophthalmology, neurology, gastroenterology, cardiovascular and dermatology. This book, as well as the other books and articles I have written, is researched and compiled with the intention to provide both veterinarians and dog owners with comprehensive and authoritative predisposition information under the breed name.

At the date of this publication, The American Kennel Club Canine Health Foundation and the The Kennel Club of England reports over 400 known hereditary health syndromes throughout the dog kingdom. At the writing of my first book in 1983, less than 50 hereditary issues are able to be predicted and or diagnosed. Sequencing of the canine genome, DNA tests, metabolic testing including blood tests and urine testing; plus, phenotypic examinations such as radiographs, ultrasound, and CERF or OFA eye registry exams by a Board Certified Veterinary Ophthalmologist have advanced the science of breed related health and behavioral problems.

This book will provide veterinarians, researchers, pet owners and breeders with a comprehensive guide to all the known problems veterinarians and dog owners should consider during pet selection and throughout each life stage of our canine friends.

NOTE

The fact that a breed shows many disorders may be more an indication of the extensive research done on that breed than on its comparative soundness of the breed.

Many genetic disorders are common to several breeds. We do not intend to convey severity of incidence by the length of text within a particular breed chapter. One breed may have forty percent incidence and another breed only four percent. If a thorough study has been done to indicate the percentage of incidence, we make note of it; however, please keep in mind the incidence is only an indicator of the dogs tested. A breed for instance may show eighteen percent incidence of hip dysplasia as indicated by OFA, although breeders and veterinarians may not elect to submit radiographs of hips so severely dysplastic that the owners and their veterinarians know that there is zero chance to be rated as OFA normal.

Please be aware that we have included and identified anecdotal information, defined by Merriam Webster's dictionary as unscientific observation; however, the observations of breeders and veterinarians with a special interest in the breed will hopefully be converted to scientific research, often underwritten by breed clubs, to confirm or rule out predisposition to breed problems.

You will note that each chapter is thoroughly referenced to help with the reader's research as well as to credit and appreciate the researchers, writers, and breeders that have helped the animal world and mankind by their work with these genetic disorders.

Ross D. Clark, D.V.M.

TABLE OF CONTENTS

GORDON SETTERS

Gordon Settler with gun and birds

ORIGIN AND HISTORY

The black and tan setter was known as far back as the 1700s. However, it became popular as a distinct breed in Scotland beginning in the early19th century, when the Duke of Gordon established a kennel. It was from this strain that the first pair, "Rake and Rachel," was brought to America in 1842 by George W. Blunt. "Rachel" was later owned by Daniel Webster. From this pair, along with other importations, an American strain of gun dog was developed. The popularity of the breed reached a height at the turn of the century when the Gordon was in demand, not only as a gentleman's shooting dog, but as the commercial hunter's favorite.

Gordon setter and Woodcocks

DESCRIPTION

The official breed Standard states: "A good-sized, sturdily-built dog, well muscled, with plenty of bone and substance, but active, up-standing and stylish, appearing capable of doing a full day's work in the field. Strong, rather short back, well sprung ribs and short tail; fairly heavy head, finely chiseled; intelligent, noble and dignified expression, showing no signs of shyness; clear colors and straight or slightly waved coat. A dog that suggests strength and stamina rather than extreme speed."

While most breeders prefer a hunting dog with show potential or a show type with hunting ability, there is a definite tendency for the hunter or field trainer to want a small or medium size dog and the show handler seems to seek to impress the judges with a larger dog. The Gordon is an affectionate, intelligent dog and responds well to obedience training. His desire to please makes him a biddable hunting companion as well as an ideal house pet. He is considered to be excellent with children.

As with all hunting breeds, the Gordon setter should not be allowed to run loose without supervision. The scent of game, or even the sight of the neighbor's cat, may cause him to start a chase that could end in tragedy.

The Gordon in the field is a close working dog, although he can be encouraged to range further ahead of the hunter as is desired in field trial competition. He quarters his ground thoroughly and seeks out likely cover. If the bird is there, he will locate it but will need some training to be "steady to wing."

Gordon setter executing the Agility Weave Polls

THE SHOW RING

In size, dogs run from 24 to 27 inches at the shoulder and 55 to 80 pounds in weight. Bitches are generally smaller, measuring 23 to 26 inches at the shoulder and 45 to 70 pounds in weight.

The color is black with tan markings. The tan should be a rich chestnut or mahogany. The locations of the tan color are specific in the standard.[1]

Predominantly tan, red or buff dogs which do not have the typical pattern of markings of a Gordon setter have a disqualifying fault. VetGen offers a direct DNA test for coat color gene variations in the Gordon setter.

Gordon Settler puppy with hunting accessories

BREEDING AND WHELPING

While the mating cycle may be variable, bitches are usually ready to breed between the 10th and 14th day of their season. Some breeders report their bitches conceive as early as the 8th day and as late as the eighteenth. The gestation period can be 58 to 65 days but is usually 61 days.

The Gordon setter litter averages eight to 12 whelps weighing 10 to 12 ounces each. Birth defects are not common. The Gordon bitch is an easy whelper and is usually able to nurse even a large litter without help.

Breeders have reported puppies born with deformities of the last two or three vertebrae of the tail.

The tan color on a puppy is obvious at birth and should deepen in color by 8 weeks. While it is not usual, a puppy can be born solid red. Some breeders destroy red puppies. While red puppies are ineligible for showing, they can now be registered with the AKC. They should not be used for breeding as the breed Standard calls for a "black and tan."

GROWTH

Kennels report an extreme range in the caloric requirements of Gordon Setters.

Gordon Setters are relatively slow to mature. Breeders expect the dog to be at its physical peak as late as 6 to 8 years of age.

RECOGNIZED RISK FACTORS IN GORDON SETTERS

CARDIOVASCULAR-HEMATOLOGICAL-RESPIRATORY

The Gordon setter is one of the breeds in which **primary ciliary dyskinesia** has been reported. [11] This condition is characterized by uncoordinated ciliary beating or the lack of beating altogether. While any ciliated organ can be affected, the most common system affected is the respiratory, with chronic disease being due to lack of mucociliary clearance.

DERMATOLOGICAL

Black hair follicular dysplasia has been recognized in the Gordon setter. [9(768), 10, 12, 20] Affected dogs are born with normal coats but the black areas begin to loose luster at about four months of age. There is a progressive loss of black hair and scaliness in affected areas with all black hair being lost by 6 to 9 months of age.

The Gordon setter is reported to be at increased risk for **inhalant allergic dermatitis (atopy)** [12] and **demodicosis** (mange). [10]

Juvenile cellulitis (Puppy strangles) is a granulomatous, pustular disorder seen in young Gordon setters. [9(1116), 10, 11, 12] Symptoms appear between 3 weeks and 4 months of age beginning with an acutely swollen face and submandibular lymphadenopathy. Papules and pustules then develop on the lips, chin, bridge of the nose and periocular area. The lesions are usually painful but not pruritic. Treatment is with large doses of glucocorticoids and antibiotics.

A type of **vitamin A responsive dermatosis**, different from the seborrheic disorder, has been observed by Kowchka, Scott et. al. in the Gordon setter. [12] Affected dogs are pruritic with papular dermatitis in the dorsal regions. Some improvement was seen with antibiotic therapy but symptoms were resolved only with continued Vitamin A administration.

Collagen disorder of the footpads has been listed as occurring in the Gordon setter. [10] Fistulous tracts appear on the plantar metatarsal surface. Both metatarsal and sometimes the metacarpal pads are involved.

Lupoid onychopathy is a term used for multiple disorders of the claws. Similarity to lupus erythematosus indicates an immune factor. Splitting and sloughing of the claws as well as brittle nails and abnormal growth are seen in one or all 18 claws. This condition has been reported in Gordon setters.[20]

ENDOCRINE-EXOCRINE-ENZYMATIC

Hypothyroidism is considered a problem in the Gordon setter [2, 10, 12] Hypothyroidism (Autoimmune Thyroiditis) is the destruction of the thyroid gland due to an attack from the animal's own immune system. Clinical signs include weight gain, lethargy, bilateral symmetric alopecia, thickened skin and hyperpigmentation. The Orthopedic Foundation for Animals (OFA) indicates that 2.0% of the Gordon setter thyroid panels submitted to its Thyroid registry is abnormal. [13]

GASTROINTESTINAL

The Gordon setter is one of the breeds at greatest risk for **gastric dilatation-volvulus**. [9(368), 10] (Bloat, Gastric Torsion, GDV) There is distension and twisting of the stomach, resulting in discomfort, vomiting and ineffectual retching with blockage of gastric outflow and circulation. Pain, shock, irregular heartbeats and death are forthcoming if not treated immediately.

MUSCULOSKELETAL

The Gordon setter has been reported to be at increased risk for **hypertrophic osteodystrophy**. [9, 10] This disease is characterized by inflammation of the metaphyses of long bones in rapidly growing puppies. Clinical signs include lameness, pain, fever, anorexia and depression with the metaphyses of the long bones, especially the forelimbs, being painful and swollen. Anti-inflammatory drugs are the treatment of choice.

Elbow dysplasia, most commonly seen as **fragmented coronoid process**, occurs in the breed. [9, 10] The OFA ranks the Gordon 28th in its registry, with 12.8 % of the elbow evaluations being abnormal. [13]

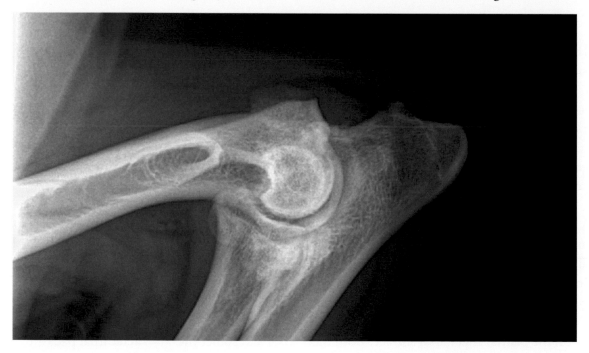

Figure 2 Elbow Dysplasia: Fragmented Coronoid Process, grade 3-Source OFA

The Gordon setter is also predisposed for **hip dysplasia**. [9, 10] The OFA ranks the breed 41st in its registry with 19.0% of the hip evaluations being abnormal. [13]

NEUROLOGIC

Epilepsy is reported to be a problem in Gordon setters. [8, 9, 10]

DUNGd (Darned unnamed genetic disease, Lethal inherited encephalopathy) was the name given to a new progressive neurologic disease first recognized in Gordon setter puppies in the late 1990s. Affected pups are born normal but begin showing neurological signs at about three weeks of age. Clinical signs begin as intermittent stiffness, weakness and tremors that become more constant as the disease progresses. The puppies will pace, circle and cry incessantly. By five to six weeks of age they cannot stand or hold their heads up and will soon die if not euthanized. Postmortem examination of nervous tissue showed little changes. It has been postulated that the condition is the result of an enzyme deficiency that results in **organic aciduria**. Amino acids, triglycerides and simple sugars are converted to energy in the brain by a process in which a series of enzymes converts a series of organic acids. If there is a deficiency of a certain enzyme, the acid to be converted will accumulate in the tissue and be excreted in abnormal amounts in the urine. Detection of that acid in the urine is an indication of which enzyme is lacking. Research is ongoing at the University of Missouri to determine the genetic basis of this condition. [17]

Cerebellar abiotrophy is a degenerative neurologic disease reported in Gordon setters. [5, 6, 7, 9, 10, 14, 15] Degeneration of Purkinje neurons in the cerebellar cortex and loss of granule neurons can occur in the breed from 6 months to 3 years of age. Early signs include forelimb stiffness, hypermetria and stumbling. There is a slowly progressing cerebellar ataxia that usually does not affect the dog's ability to stand. The condition is inherited as an autosomal recessive trait. Dr. Natasha Olby of North Carolina State University has isolated the mutation causing cerebellar abiotrophy in Gordon setters and the NCSU Veterinary Genetics Lab offers a DNA test to determine clear, carrier and affected states in the breed.

OPHTHALMIC

Eyelid disorders found in the Gordon setter include: **distichiasis** [16] (abnormally located eyelashes along the lid margin), **ectropion** (eversion of the eyelids) [16] and lower eyelid **entropion** [9(350), 10, 16] (in rolling of the eyelid). All of these disorders can result in ocular irritation. Entropion and ectropion are the result of multiple factors including amount and weight of skin on the head, contents of the orbit and the shape of the skull.

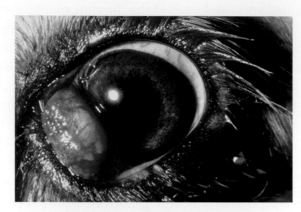

Ectropion

Distichiasis, note the presence of eyelashes directed toward the cornea.

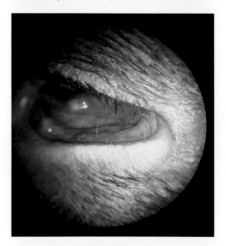

Entropion

Medial canthal pocket syndrome occurs in Gordon setters. [10] Deep orbits and a mild entropion lead to poor drainage of tears and chronic conjunctivitis.

The Gordon setter is one of the breeds most often affected with **keratoconjunctivitis sicca (KCS, dry eye)**. [9(1119), 10] KCS is an abnormality of the aqueous portion of the tear film usually caused by an immune mediated attack on the lacrimal glands causing a reduction of tear production and ocular irritation.

Persistent pupillary membranes (PPM) have been recognized in Gordon setters.[16] PPM are vascular remnants that have failed to regress existing in the anterior chamber of the eye. They may form bridges from the iris to the iris, the iris to the lens or cornea or form sheets in the anterior chamber. The number and location determine if they can cause vision impairment. All forms of PPM have been found in Gordon setters.

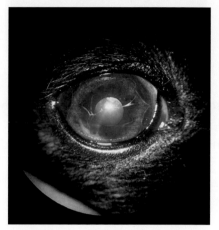

Persistent Pupillary Membranes-PPM

Iris cysts have been reported in the breed. [16] These cysts are formed from the posterior pigmented cells of the iris. They may remain attached or break free and float as pigmented spheres in the anterior chamber.

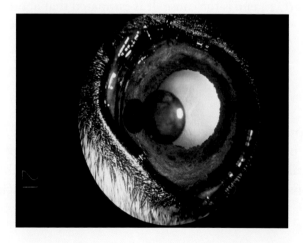

Iris Cysts

Cataracts have been reported in the Gordon setter. [9(903), 10, 16] A cataract is defined as any opacity of the lens and/or its capsule that when complete will cause blindness in the affected eye.

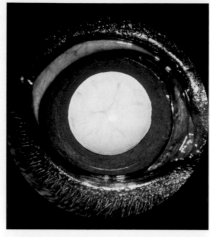

Cataract

Micropapilla [9(903)] and **persistent hyaloid artery** [16] have both been reported in the Gordon setter. Micropapilla refers to a small optic disk that does not affect vision. The persistent hyaloid is a vascular remnant in the vitreous chamber that has been linked to cataracts and retinal detachment.

Retinal dysplasia (folds) has been reported in Gordon setters. [9(350), 10, 16] Multiple areas of linear, curved or triangular folds are seen in the retinas of affected dogs. These folds may correct as the dog matures and do not appear to affect vision.

The Gordon setter is predisposed for early-onset **Progressive retinal atrophy (PRA)**. [3, 4, 9(827), 10, 16] Clinical signs can begin between 3 and 12 months of age with the condition being inherited as an autosomal recessive trait. There are at least two forms of PRA in the Gordon setter. The one designated rcd4 is the most common. Rcd4-PRA is a late-onset disease with the average age of onset being10 to 12 years. A mutation of the C2orf71 gene is the cause. It is estimated that about 18% of the Gordon setters in the USA carry this mutation. Animal Health Trust, UK, Optigen and the OFA offer a DNA test for rcd4 in the Gordon setter. [21, 25]

BEHAVIOR

The Gordon is very adaptable to guarding and family life. He is sincere, helpful and polite. He is very affectionate with his family but can be reserved with strangers. A survey of Gordon owners in Germany characterized the breed as calm, stable and friendly as well as being sociable with other dogs and easily trained. [22] Other sources consider them slightly willful with slight tendencies toward dog and territorial aggression. [23]

OLD AGE

The average life span of the Gordon is 12 years. A survey of the Veterinary Medical Database lists gastrointestinal problems and cancer as the most commonly diagnosed causes of death in the breed. [19] The Health and Genetics Committee of the Gordon Setter Club of America lists bloat and four types of cancer in its Health Concerns list. [20]

MISCELLANEOUS FACTS AND RESOURCES

This is a list of Genetic tests available for the Gordon setter to identify inherited medical problems that may be recommended by your Veterinarian.

GENETIC TESTS AVAILABLE FOR THE GORDON SETTER

Condition	Laboratory
Cerebellar Abiotrophy	NC State Vet. Genetics Lab
Coat Color Determination	VetGen
Progressive Retinal Atrophy (rcd4)	Animal Health Trust, UK, OFA, Laboklin, UK, Optigen

For information about the laboratories performing these tests and sample submission contact:

www.offa.org/dna_labs.html

Additional health screening tests recommended for the Gordon setter by the Canine Health Information Center (CHIC)

Here is how CHIC works to help dog fanciers improve their breeds

CHIC works with national breed clubs, the AKC Canine Health Foundation and the Orthopedic Foundation for Animals (OFA) to create a list of health screening procedures designed to eliminate inherited health problems from dogs used for breeding. The procedures vary from breed to breed and may change if new problems are identified or new tests become available. A dog must have completed all the required health screening procedures in order to receive a CHIC number. For more information contact: www.caninehealthinfo.org/

CHIC REQUIREMENTS FOR THE GORDON SETTER

Hip Dysplasia: OFA, OVC or PennHip evaluation
Elbow Dysplasia: OFA or OVC evaluation
Eye Exam by a boarded ACVO Ophthalmologist: Results registered with CERF or OFA
Rcd4 Progressive Retinal Atrophy: OFA evaluation of a DNA test from an approved laboratory
DNA Repository: Participation in the CHIC/OFA DNA Repository [18]

NATIONAL BREED CLUB

The National Breed Club is a good place to discover all the things you can do with your Gordon setter and to contact other Gordon setter owners.

GORDON SETTER CLUB OF AMERICA, INC.

www.gsca.org

REFERENCES

1. American Kennel Club, *The Complete Dog Book*. 18th ed. (Howell Book House Inc., New York, N.Y., 1992) 79-83.
2. Scott, C.W. and Paradis, M. "A Survey of Canine and Feline Skin Disorders Seen in a University Practice," Small Animal Clinic, University of Montreal, Saint-Hyacinth, Quebec, 1987-l 988: *Can. Vet. Jour.* 1990: 31:12, 835-839; 50 refs.
3. Hodgman, S.F.J., Parry, H.B., Rasbridge, W.J. and Steel, J.D. "Progressive Retinal Atrophy in Dogs I: The Disease in Irish Setters (Red)," *Vet. Rec.*; 1949: 61:185-l 90.
4. Magnusson, H. "About Retinitis Pigmentosa and Consanguinity in Dogs," *Arch. Vergh. Uphthal*; 1911: 2:147-163.
5. De LaHunta, A., Fenner, W.R., Indrieri, R.J. *et al*, "Hereditary Cerebellar Cortical Abiotrophy in the Gordon Setter," *JAVMA*; Sept., 1980: 177:538-541.
6. Gorham, M.E. "Brittany Spaniels and Gordon Setters Plagued by Hereditary Muscle Disease," *DVM*; March, 1982: 13(3):52-54.
7. Ettinger, S.J. *Textbook of Veterinary Medicine*, Diseases of the Dog and Cat. W.B. Saunders, Co. Philadelphia, PA. 1989: 597-598.
8. Bell, Jerold S. DVM "Sex Related Genetic Disorders: Did Mama Cause Them?" *American Kennel Club Gazette*, Feb. 1994; 76.
9. Ackerman, Lowell, The Genetic Connection: a Guide to Health Problems in Purebred Dogs. Lakewood, AAHA Press, 1999.
10. Padgett, George A. Control of Canine Genetic Diseases. New York, Howell Book House. 1998
11. Tilley, Lawrence P., Smith, Francis W.K. Hr. The 5 Minute Veterinary Consult; Canine and Feline, 3rd ed. Baltimore, Lippencott Williams and Wilkins. 2004
12. Scott, Danny W., Miller, William H. Jr., Griffin, Craig E. Muller and Kirk's Small Animal Dermatology-6th ed. Philadelphia, W.B. Saunders Co. 2001
13. Orthopedic Foundation for Animals website: www.offa.org
14. Coates, Joan R., Kline, Karen L. Congenital and Inherited Neurologic Disorders in Dogs and Cats. p. 1113 Kirk's Current Veterinary Therapy XII. Philadelphia, W>B> Saunders Co. 1995
15. Lorenz, Michael d., Korngay Joe N. Handbook of Veterinary Neurology, 4th ed. Philadelphia, W.B. Saunders Co. 2004
16. Genetics Committee of the American College of Veterinary Ophthalmologists, Ocular Disorders Presumed to be Inherited in Purebred Dogs, 5th ed. 2009
17. DUNGd A Fatal Neonatal Disease of Gordon Setters. Canine Genetic Diseases Network: www.caninegeneticdiseases.net/DUNGd/DUNGd.htm
18. Gordon Setter Breed Requirements, Canine Health Information center: www.caninehealthinfo.org
19. Health Concerns, Gordon Setter Health & Genetics Committee: http//gsca.org/health/index.html
20. Bohnhorst, J.O., Hanssen, I., Moen, T. Antinuclear antibodies (ANA) in Gordon setters with symmetrical lupoid onychodystrophy and black hair follicular dysplasia. Acta Vet Scand, 2001; 42:232-9
21. Progressive Retinal Atrophy in Gordon setter; Animal Health Trust www.aht.org.uk/cms-display/genetics_prarcd4.html
22. Turcsan, B., Kubinyi, E. Miklosi, A. Trainability and boldness traits differ between dog breed clusters based on conventional breed categories and genetic relatedness Appl Anim Behav Sci 2011 132:61-70
23. Gordon Setters; Vetstreet: www.vetstreet.com/dogs/gordon-setter
24. Neurogenetic laboratory; Veterinary Genetics laboratory, North Carolina State University: www.cvm.ncsu.edu/vhc/csd/vcgl/index.html.
25. rcd4 (Late onset PRA) test now available Optigen website: www.optigen.com/opt9_rcd4PRA.html

Printed in the United States
By Bookmasters